# LIFE LESSONS IN LEADERSHIP:
## THE WAY OF THE WALLABY

### FOR LEADERS AGES 8 TO 88

Compliments of:

**BIG DEAL MEDIA**
Trusted Resources for Educators

Library of Congress Control Number: 2016914952
CreateSpace Independent Publishing Platform, North Charleston, SC

ISBN-13: 978-1537237619
ISBN-10: 1537237616

## Acknowledgments

The authors, Ann McMullan and Michael Barrett, wish to extend sincere thanks to the talented friends and colleagues who contributed to the creation of *Life Lessons in Leadership: The Way of the Wallaby.*

### Becky Benavides, Writer & Broadcast Producer

Without Becky, this book would never have come to life. Becky is the ultimate "connector" who brought everyone together. She follows the Way of the Wallaby whenever and however she can. That's because Becky firmly believes that bringing the right people together for the right reasons can make wonderful, meaningful things happen. In this case, it began by introducing Ann to Sheila and Josephine. And then to Michael, Lisa, and Jim. The rest was simply wallaby wisdom at work—and play.

### Jim Feeley, Character Designer & Illustrator

We are beyond grateful for Jim's outstanding talent and skills. His lively character designs for Sheila and Josephine created a visual representation of these pivotal creatures in an original story by Michael Barrett. Without his vision and artistry, no one would know what the wallabies look like.

### Joe Russo II and James A. Fino

Joe and James are both gifted animation producers and close friends and supporters of Sheila and Josephine. Without their help you - our readers - wouldn't be able to see Sheila and Josephine in visual form. And you'd never know how cute they are.

### And finally…

Thank you to all those who modeled servant leadership to us throughout our lives: our parents, teachers, community leaders and professional colleagues. Immeasurable gratitude and appreciation goes out to the people we have had the privilege of leading over the course of our lives, including, but not limited to, our siblings, classmates, children, students and the professional colleagues we have encountered in our life journeys. Each of them - in their own way - taught us our life lessons in leadership which we are now happy to share with you.

# TABLE OF CONTENTS:

# LIFE LESSONS IN LEADERSHIP:

## THE WAY OF THE WALLABY

FOR LEADERS AGES 8 TO 88

# INTRODUCTION

In the fast changing, hyper-connected world of the 21st century, it is a given that at some point in your life the opportunity or responsibility of leading others will fall on your shoulders. *Though an ever growing number of people do serve as leaders, not all possess the skill sets to lead effectively.* It may happen that some of those skills come naturally as a part of an individual's personality. Other times the prerequisite skills must be learned in order to have a positive impact on the people and processes surrounding anyone's leadership. Throughout this book, the ideas about leadership always fall under the concept of "servant leadership." True leaders – in any capacity – strive to make those around them successful. When they do that, they serve the people they are leading.

*Serving as a leader can start at an early age.* It may simply be by virtue of the fact that you are the oldest sibling in your family. As you go through school you may take on student leadership roles in a classroom, on the sports field, in a band or other school organizations. Leaders are more commonly recognized in their adult leadership roles with titles like teacher, principal, pastor, director, manager, administrator, superintendent, CEO, commander, or president. Additionally, being a parent is one of the most critical leadership roles in any society.

Whatever leadership role you find yourself in, there are basic principles of leadership that will strengthen your abilities and help to assure your success. This book seeks to define those skills by making them clear and easily understood. By combining literary text with captivating stories, leaders of all ages have the opportunity to learn life lessons in leadership in ways that are not only meaningful and memorable but also engaging, entertaining and enchanting.

**I**NTRODUCING THE WALLABIES: SHEILA & JOSEPHINE.

Sheila and Josephine, fuzzy with fur,
Looked just like small kangaroos--which they were.
Sheila, with natural wisdom and bravery,
Taught Josie everything, such as which savory
Leaves and fruits settled the best in her tummy
To grow strong and smart, and not just the most yummy.

Josie lay sometimes curled up in mom's pouch
But don't be deceived. This girl was no slouch.
They hopped through the world and supported each other,
Now teaching, now learning--a child and a mother.
What kind of leaders can wallabies be?
The natural kind, as the reader will see.

JOSIE

SHEILA

# CHAPTER 1: LISTEN

When serving as a leader for others, whether in a family, classroom, business, civic or any other environment, *listening is the most critical skill*. A leader cannot know the full scope of all the issues that impact the effort she is leading on her own. For that reason a leader must depend on family members, colleagues and associates or whomever she is leading, in order to gather necessary information and collaborate on strategies and solutions. People often perceive that a leader's job is to give orders. That may - in rare instances - be true, but it cannot be the first order of business for a leader.

*Listening must come first.*

The ability to truly listen – not simply to hear – is a leader's most important skill. It is through active, engaged listening that a leader begins to understand the reality of what is truly going on with both the people and processes she is leading. *Listening has to be followed by appropriate action in order for the leader to maintain legitimacy with others.* The combined efforts of effective listening and appropriate follow-up action will serve everyone well by contributing to an atmosphere of trust in which everyone can flourish.

Is Anyone Listening?

CONSIDER THE CASE OF POOR SEPTIMUS GEEZER
IN TRYING TO MOLD HIS UNPAID INTERN, WHEEZER.
"Wheezer!" said Geezer.
"Take charge of the coffee
And furnish this meeting with sweet rolls and toffee."

Frantically looking through cupboards devoid
Of these items, and getting dismayed and annoyed,
Wheezer returned to the ear of his boss
And whispered, "I'm sorry, it may not be poss--"

"There's no 'i' in can't," said his boss with a sniff.
"The aroma of failure is what I won't whiff.
Nothing good comes to the whining excuser
Who lets standards fall ever lower and looser."

Having no time to get out to a store,
Wheezer ransacked every closet and drawer
In the building for all kinds of substitute stuff--
Seven stale crackers and cocoa with snuff.

With a look of deep pain, Geezer pondered the mystery
Of how he kept hiring the worst help in history.

AT THAT VERY MOMENT, ELSEWHERE IN THE WORLD,
JOSEPHINE LAY IN HER MOTHER'S POUCH CURLED
AND ASKED, "HOW'S IT, MOTHER, ALL DAY, EVERY DAY,
YOU KNOW THE EXACT TIMES TO EAT, TALK AND PLAY?"

Sheila, her mom, replied, "Actually, YOU
Let me know when it's time for the next thing we do.
You get tired, you get hungry, you get super-jumpy,
You're funny, you're happy, you're blue, and you're grumpy.

I just pay attention and get my next cue,
My own little dear one, by LISTENING TO YOU.

HEY!

# CHAPTER 2: LEARN

There is a very close correlation between listening and learning when it comes to effective leadership. Though not the only way a leader learns, *listening to those you are leading is critical to any leader's ability to learn.*

In today's world, where everything changes so rapidly, the ability to admit that you need to learn more and then act on that need to learn is essential to effective leadership. Modeling ongoing professional learning and being willing to change course when new knowledge is gained is something all followers need to see in their leaders. In the past under a more stringent top down leadership model, subordinates may have thought – or been forced to assume – that the boss knew all the answers, or else he would not have been given the position of boss. Today we know that collaboration, communication, critical thinking and creative problem solving are skill sets that all workers must possess, and leaders most of all.

True leaders often have to deal with complex issues in order to successfully navigate change. The reality is that navigating change gets to the essence of leadership. Keeping things exactly as they are may require good management but rarely requires real leadership.

In the speech he wrote and planned to give in Dallas in November 1963, President John F. Kennedy stated, *"...leadership and learning are indispensable to each other."* Kennedy's wisdom resonates even more strongly today. Being an engaged, active, life-long learner is a prerequisite to success as a leader in any environment.

"ALL RIGHT, IT'S DECIDED," SAID IVAN DUBROVNIK
IN MEETING WITH CELL MEMBERS PLOTNIK AND SLOVNIK.

After much study, debate and report
On the matter of whether it's safe to resort
To push-button telephones in place of rotary,
Finally the motion was carried by votary.

"But steer clear of cellphones, and Internet too,
Until we've heard back from the boys at HQ."
"It's 25 years since we've heard," mentioned Slovnik.
"And what is your hurry?" asked Comrade Dubrovnik.

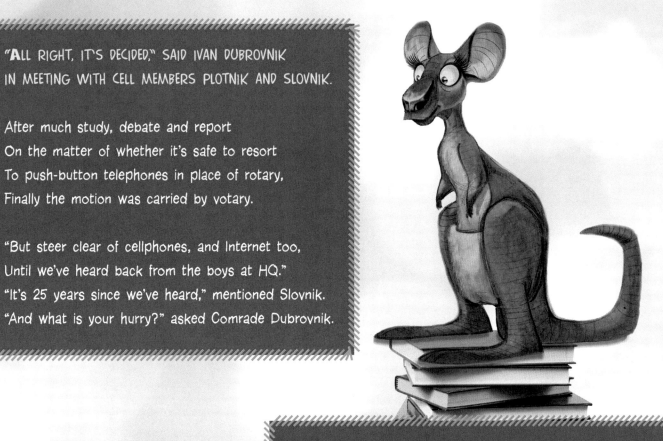

"WHAT DO KIDS MEAN," JOSIE SAID TO HER MOTHER,
"ABOUT TEXTING AND TUBING AND TWITCHING EACH OTHER?"
"It sounds kind of interesting. What have you heard?"
Asked Sheila, who wanted to know every word.

Before very long, with some trial and error
And research and questions, and no time for terror
Of strange innovations, and finding the library
Gave them all info for free without bribery,

Josie and Sheila were linking and sharing--
Without too much surfing, nor much solitairing--
And discovering previously unguessed-at tools
For making new friends just like networking fools.

The more that they learned, the more they perceived,
Until OTHERS were asking THEM!

WHO'D HAVE BELIEVED?

# CHAPTER 3: LOVE

Effective leaders function with authenticity when they humbly view their roles as servant leaders. *Impactful leaders know they must direct their focus outside themselves by truly loving the program, process and people they are leading.* Leadership requires passion in order to face ambiguities and forge a path that others will follow. Without genuine zeal for both the program and the people, insincerity and "faking it" become disturbingly clear to everyone involved. A leader's fervent commitment is evident when the listening and learning skills described in the previous chapters are obvious to all.

Empathy, thoughtfulness and compassion all play a part in the way leaders who love carry out their leadership functions. When loving leaders make decisions, they actively consider how their actions affect those they are leading. Leaders also recognize that conflict and resistance are a natural part of moving any organization or team forward. *Responding to conflict and resistance from a loving perspective – rather than a dictatorial, power-based approach -* goes a long way in assuring that those who follow you will support your efforts with their loyalty and commitment.

Having a loving attitude toward all the people in your family, team, department, organization, etc. is a strong motivator for your colleagues. As a leader you do not have to like everyone you are leading, but you must have their best interests at heart. A leader should care enough and love enough to want everyone involved to succeed. However, success is not always guaranteed. Mistakes happen and the way a leader deals with her own mistakes or the mistakes of others has to be rooted in love for the people and the purpose and goals of the team or organization. Caring love provides support, encouragement and guidance that comes from the heart, not the bottom line.

BARRINGTON BARRINGTON JR., ESQUIRE,
FELT DRIVEN BY LOVE TO CONTROL AN EMPIRE.
He loved leading underlings, guiding them through,
Dispensing strict orders on what they must do.

He loved being focus of all their attention
And loved holding patents on every invention
Or formula, process, or plan they suggested,
And loved most of all when they just genuflected.

He was so full of love, he could burst into song.
It's no mystery why no one stayed with him long.

WHILE SKYLARKING OUT WITH THEIR WALLABY CLAN,

Josephine shyly suggested a plan
For gathering berries out there in the wild
And planting more bushes for later. "Why, child,"
Said Sheila, "let's show all the others
How it can be smarter for kiddos and mothers
To organize patches of ground for the gobbling
And maybe lean seasons won't leave us so hobbling."

It took not much effort by gesture and letter
When all wanted everyone's lives to be better.
They took to the plan and, no matter who said it,
They all *loved* the job and they ALL GOT THE CREDIT.

# CHAPTER 4: LEVERAGE

*Leveraging the talents of others to support the vision and goals of a family or team is critical to the success of any leader's endeavors.* Leaders who listen, learn and love both the people and the program they guide know they cannot possibly accomplish everything on their own. It is through active listening that leaders become aware of the talents and skills of those around them.

Kathy Hurley, co-founder and CEO of Girls Thinking Global, and co-editor of *Real Women, Real Leaders*: *Surviving and Succeeding in the Business World*, has shared her wisdom on leveraging and maximizing the talents of others in both private conversations and public venues. Hurley's artful advice is paraphrased here:

1. Jobs and situations may change but people do not. Do not burn bridges as you move from one assignment or role to another.
2. Network, even when you don't have to. The person you meet today may turn out to be a valued confidant or colleague in another setting at some point in the future.
3. Always err on the side of generosity. Help others, even when there is no immediate benefit or reward for yourself.

*Leveraging others' talents does not mean delegating all the work to other people.* Leadership by its very nature is a collaborative effort. Associates will neither thrive nor produce well if they perceive that their leader does nothing more than assign all tasks to others. A leader must model an exceptional work ethic. Empowered leaders depend not only on the talents of others, but also on their own talents as well.

Leveraging time - as well as talent - is a skill set that all leaders must develop. Regardless of our role in life we are each only given the same twenty-four hours in a day. It is therefore incumbent upon a leader to prioritize her use of time. And there will be times when setting priorities has to be done on the fly. Therefore schedules must guide, but not rule the day. At the same time, flexibility should not be confused with distractions.

When it comes to managing time a truly effective leader must always strive for balance in her life. *To lead others well, an effective leader must also be a whole, complete person.* When a leader's focus is always exclusively on her leadership role, she denies those who follow her the collegiality of a well-adjusted, stable person.

Barrington's enterprise ended in bankruptcy
Thanks to absconding execs of corruptancy,

Causing much soul-searching inside the boss--
Though his parachute left him less worse for the loss
Than all those poor saps now left laid off and jobless
Without any benefits even to sob less.

"I've learned now," said he. "I should take any lengths
To buy the best people, applying their strengths
As each one does best, to run each division
In harmony with my elaborate vision,
In this way achieving my singular goal
Of fitting each part into my perfect whole.

The crucial point is to let no employee
Have more money, ideas or power than me."

When tending their garden, the wallabies found
Some would dig deeper, some covered more ground,
Some of the lighter ones were higher jumpers,
Some of the others were heavier thumpers,

Smaller claw-fingers were delicate pickers,
While tougher paws handled the nettles and stickers.
Sheila would hint, recommend and suggest,
Because all were happiest doing their best.

Their talents got *leveraged* each to their action,
And that sense of USEFULNESS BREEDS SATISFACTION.

# CHAPTER 5: LUCK

The *Merriam-Webster Dictionary* defines luck as "a force that brings good fortune or adversity" and "the events or circumstances that operate for or against an individual."

When you consider the impact of luck on people's actions, two elements come to mind:

1. Having the ability to leverage luck means that ***you work to prepare yourself to be ready to respond to luck when it appears.*** There are times in life when opportunity presents itself, but if you are not ready nor prepared, opportunity will pass you by. Wise leaders know that practice, preparation and staying keenly aware of circumstances and changes puts you in a position to grab luck and maximize opportunities when they come your way. "Do your homework" is not just an admonition for students in school. Leadership always requires prep work. Effective leaders understand that preparation is a process which must always be thorough and ongoing.

2. The "force" that *Merriam-Webster* refers to is usually the leader herself. When others view a leader's success they may mistakenly chalk it up to "good luck." What others see as luck should more appropriately be viewed as having the right perspective in good times and bad. ***When unfortunate events occur, wise leaders use those times as opportunities to grow and learn*** and thereby turn their "bad luck" into good. The reality is that leaders who listen, learn, love and leverage talent and time are truly creating their own luck.

Sheila was constantly sought for advice
To help their new garden in shaping up nice.
One or two wallabies weren't great at such labors.
She put them in charge of liaising with neighbors
Along hills and valleys for possible trade,
And that's how they founded the PR Brigade.

First the deer families, then warrens of rabbits,
Were gently persuaded that changing their habits
Of simply devouring the wallabies' fruits
Could prove beneficial as new leaves and roots
Yielded more good for their wild community,
Increasing their food and decreasing disunity.

High in the trees, all this bustle and growth
Attracted attention from one three-toed sloth
Who opened one eye on these happy and plucky
Producers, and sighed, and thought, "SOME ARE BORN LUCKY."

# EPILOGUE: LEAD

The intent of this book is to provide leaders of all ages with quick reference points to guide their paths to success in any leadership role. Equally important is the concept of educating our readers through entertaining stories cleverly written in enchanting verse. The voices of the lovable wallabies, Sheila and Josephine, and their associated characters charmingly illustrate both how and why the ability to intentionally *listen, learn, love, leverage time and talent, and create and optimize luck, are vital skills for anyone in a leadership role.*

Beyond the five "L's" covered in this book one could also add *laughter and living life to its fullest.* The ability to laugh at yourself and to laugh with others (never at them) generates feelings of endearment and mutual respect. Living life to the fullest allows leaders to find equilibrium within all parts of their lives. When done well, leaders operate with poise and steadiness that inspires all those around them to be and do their very best.

### ANN MCMULLAN
*Education Consultant, Public Speaker, Author*

Ann McMullan is the founder and lead consultant of her own education consulting firm, based in Los Angeles, California, who understands leadership firsthand from her sixteen years of leading innovative change in Klein ISD, a fast growing dynamic school district in the Houston, Texas, area. Ann serves education leaders, teachers, nonprofits and firms doing business with schools and school districts to advise and assist with their leadership and strategic planning work. She facilitates leadership workshops, both face to face and via webinars. As a recognized thought leader in her field, Ann is a frequent contributor to education journals and newsletters. Ann's public speaking engagements include international, national and state conference keynotes, workshops, breakout sessions and panel presentations on leading the transformation of learning and teaching to meet the needs of today's students, teachers and administrators.

For more information, or to contact Ann McMullan, please visit:
LifeLessonsInLeadership.com or annmcmullan.com.

### LISA BRESHEARS
*Art Director & Graphic Designer*

Lisa grew up while traveling and living in all sorts of places because of her father's military career. She attended college in San Antonio, Texas, where she majored in Fine Arts/Advertising. Her career as an advertising art director and graphic designer has been a notable one. Lisa's work has won multiple awards in local, regional, and national creative competitions. After working in ad agencies for many years, Lisa decided to open her own creative services company. Her art direction and design for this book make it enjoyable to look at, while visually enhancing the story.

For more information, or to contact Lisa Breshears, please visit:
LifeLessonsInLeadership.com.

## MICHAEL BARRETT
*Free-lance writer*

Michael Barrett is a free-lance writer, born and residing in San Antonio, Texas. He attended that city's Trinity University and University of California at Davis. His film articles and reviews can be found in *Video Watchdog*, *Nostalgia Digest* and *PopMatters.com*. Michael has written creatively about wallabies, zeppelins, penguins, poltergeists, skunks, extraterrestrials, and all manner of joy and devilment. He offers his services to write on demand.

For more information, or to contact Michael Barrett, please visit: LifeLessonsInLeadership.com.

THE END

Made in the USA
Lexington, KY
01 July 2019